T0003311

Atoms Everywhere!

Unpeeled by **Russ** and **Yammy**
with **Nury Vittachi**
Illustrated by **Alan Bay**

WS Education

NEW JERSEY · LONDON · SINGAPORE · BEIJING · SHANGHAI · HONG KONG · TAIPEI · CHENNAI · TOKYO

Published by

WS Education, an imprint of
World Scientific Publishing Co. Pte. Ltd.
5 Toh Tuck Link, Singapore 596224
USA office: 27 Warren Street, Suite 401-402, Hackensack, NJ 07601
UK office: 57 Shelton Street, Covent Garden, London WC2H 9HE

British Library Cataloguing-in-Publication Data
A catalogue record for this book is available from the British Library.

Science Everywhere!
ATOMS EVERYWHERE!
Unpeeled by Russ and Yammy with Nury Vittachi

ISBN 978-981-124-898-6 (hardcover)
ISBN 978-981-124-979-2 (paperback)
ISBN 978-981-124-899-3 (ebook for institutions)
ISBN 978-981-124-904-4 (ebook for individuals)

Desk Editor: Amanda Yun
Illustrator: Alan Bay

Printed in Singapore

CONTENTS

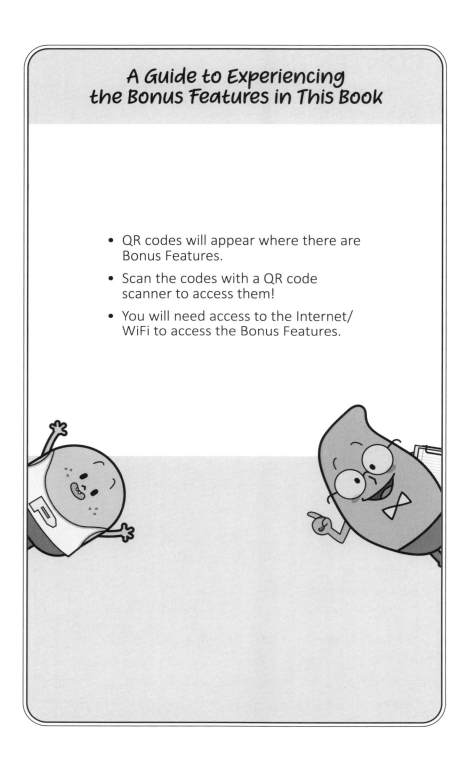

A Guide to Experiencing the Bonus Features in This Book

- QR codes will appear where there are Bonus Features.
- Scan the codes with a QR code scanner to access them!
- You will need access to the Internet/WiFi to access the Bonus Features.

Reading Guide

Before we begin, look out for these headers for a quick start to your journey with us!

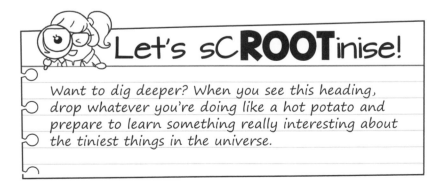

Fact Snack

Get the low down on the most fascinating facts about atoms whenever you see this header – tasty and bite-sized!

Let's sCROOTinise!

Want to dig deeper? When you see this heading, drop whatever you're doing like a hot potato and prepare to learn something really interesting about the tiniest things in the universe.

Chapter 1

Every year you get atoms for your birthday!

Here's a trick. Close your eyes for a moment and imagine you are holding several hundred grams of the strangest, most magical substance in the universe. Now open your eyes wide and make a discovery: you actually are. Yep. It's this book. It's made of the most puzzling, intriguing elements in the universe: atoms. They are not just small, ball-shaped objects. They do lots of extraordinary things – including flickering in and out of existence, and travelling in time!

Fact Snack

If someone asks you what you're doing, you can reply, "Oh, just studying NUCLEAR PHYSICS." That impressive-sounding phrase is the ACTUAL scientific name for the study of atoms.

It's not rocket science. Wait. Maybe it is.

And of course, it's not just the book. Your chair and your table are made of atoms, as are your hands, with which you are using to hold this volume. Even the light that's travelling between the page and your eyes is made up of tiny, tiny particles, shooting into your eyes. (Luckily, they are not itchy.)

Tater Toons

Fact Snack

Atoms are so teeny-weeny that you would need to put at least 200,000 of them side by side to add up to the width of a single strand of hair.

Atoms hide an astonishing secret. People think they are literally the tiniest, puniest, most miniscule things in the universe. But it's all a trick! An atom is actually a super powerful thing: it is stronger than your favourite superhero, louder than your favourite music group, and has more impact than the biggest lightning storm on the planet. That's because atoms contain unbelievable amounts of hidden energy. Cut them and the energy escapes, causing huge explosions.

Fact Snack

Nuclear explosions producing massive mushroom-shaped clouds that fill the sky come from the splitting of tiny atoms. Atoms deserve RESPECT.

Let's scROOTinise!

Atoms make up every object that exists, including human beings — yet they were the biggest mystery in science for millenniums.

Some of the greatest scientific thinkers of history, including Plato and Aristotle, did not believe in them, so you currently know more than they did!

Even in modern times, Albert Einstein spent years arguing with other scientists about atoms, and the tiny particles seemed to outwit him regularly. He felt that descriptions of their behaviour made it sound like they did things that were impossible in science. The trouble was that experiments showed that these time-travelling, space-hopping balls of something WERE doing the impossible.

Where do atoms hide all their fabled amounts of energy? After all, if they're so small, there can't be a lot of room inside, surely? True. The energy is tucked into the forces that hold them together. We'll look for the hidden energy later in this book.

Also in this book, we'll look at how exactly you can go about splitting an atom, but you'll have to PROMISE not to make a working nuclear reactor on your kitchen table. It may be illegal and it definitely will be a big, messy job that could seriously annoy your mum or dad. Promise? Okay.

Yikes! I wonder if stain remover removes radioactive waste?

Now you may already know that there are different types of atoms, and that they make up things called elements. There's probably a chart on the wall at school showing this. But did you know that you can MAKE a new atomic element yourself? Making new elements is not an easy job, but several people have done it. There are 92 natural elements, but the list goes up to 118 if we include ones that people have made. Otherwise, you could make new molecules (combinations of atoms), which are a bit easier.

PERIODIC TABLE OF ELEMENTS																	
H																	He
Li	Be			H	Symbol						B	C	N	O	F	Ne
Na	Mg											Al	Si	P	S	Cl	Ar
K	Ca	Sc	Ti	V	Cr	Mn	Fe	Co	Ni	Cu	Zn	Ga	Ge	As	Se	Br	Kr
Rb	Sr	Y	Zr	Nb	Mo	Tc	Ru	Rh	Pd	Ag	Cd	In	Sn	Sb	Te	I	Xe
Cs	Ba		Hf	Ta	W	Re	Os	Ir	Pt	Au	Hg	Tl	Pb	Bi	Po	At	Rn
Fr	Ra		Rf	Db	Sg	Bh	Hs	Mt	Ds	Rg	Cn	Nh	Fl	Mc	Lv	Ts	Og
		La	Ce	Pr	Nd	Pm	Sm	Eu	Gd	Tb	Dy	Ho	Er	Tm	Yb	Lu	
		Ac	Th	Pa	U	Np	Pu	Am	Cm	Bk	Cf	Es	Fm	Md	No	Lr	

Let's sC**ROOT**inise!

Combinations of atoms make very small objects called molecules, and chemists sometimes make new ones and give them funny names.

Angelic Acid doesn't sing or wear white clothes. It's the name of an acid made from a flower called Angelic. There's also a compound called Megaphone, which has nothing to do with loudspeakers.

One molecule is commonly known as Penguinone, because some chemists think it looks like a penguin. Here's a picture of it next to a penguin (for comparison). Do you think it looks like a penguin?

I think you're spending too much time in the gym...

!!!

The study of atoms includes the study of the bits that make up atoms, which we call subatomic (meaning "smaller-than-an-atom") particles. And those very, very small items are even more fascinating and mysterious. These are the elements that do the really cool stuff, sometimes defying the rules of space and time! For example, we all agree that your head is made of atoms, and so is your brain. But what about your thoughts? Some scientists say that it appears that thoughts could be made of subatomic particles too!

Do you know what is the strangest thing of all about atoms? They seem to have found a way of assembling themselves into objects that can study themselves! Really. Think of it this way. The universe itself is actually a very, very large collection of atoms. You are a group of atoms, studying a book about atoms, written and illustrated and published by other groups of atoms. So the atoms that make up this universe have literally found a way to study themselves. Pretty clever for such small objects!

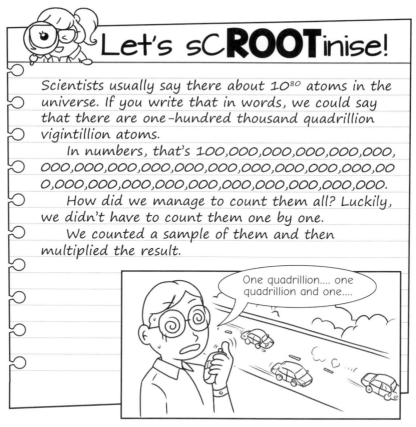

Let's scROOTinise!

Scientists usually say there about 10^{80} atoms in the universe. If you write that in words, we could say that there are one-hundred thousand quadrillion vigintillion atoms.

In numbers, that's 100,000,000,000,000,000, 000,000,000,000,000,000,000,000,000,000,00 0,000,000,000,000,000,000,000,000,000,000.

How did we manage to count them all? Luckily, we didn't have to count them one by one.

We counted a sample of them and then multiplied the result.

One quadrillion.... one quadrillion and one....

If you want to amaze your friends (or adults you know) by explaining to them exactly how small an atom is, scan the QR code on the left to go to an educational video which explains it well.

One of the nice things about the story of atoms is that there are some wonderful characters who helped us discover them, and we'll start meeting them in the next chapter. While most discoveries happen in a single moment, or over a series of days or weeks, the discovery of atoms took more than two millenniums – more than 2,000 years!

It all started a very, very long time ago with a man who was not a scientist in the modern sense at all. If anything, he was a bit of a comedian. Was he joking when he came up with the idea that the world was made of tiny multi-functional building bricks? Let's travel back in time and ask him.

Chapter 2

What if you kept cutting something in half forever?

The first scientists didn't wear white coats and work in laboratories. They were thinkers who sat under trees, looked up at the stars, and thought about stuff.

Despite not having microscopes, laboratories or telescopes, they made huge numbers of great discoveries and laid the foundations of physics, chemistry and biology. Modern science can be said to have developed out of a branch of "professional thinking" known as natural philosophy, which means developing ideas about the natural world.

The word "scientist" and the word "physicist" were not coined until the 1800s, and both were invented by a British priest-scientist-teacher named William Whewell, who wrote science books, poetry, sermons and lectures – all of them rather well.

To save time, I'll be preaching a rhyming sermon on a scientific academic topic. It's called: 'There once was an atom from Chatham'.

The recorded history of atoms can be traced back to the great sage Aruni, who lived in India 2,800 years ago, and who tackled one of the biggest philosophical questions: What is the nature of matter? We can think of this philosophical question more simply, like this: Hey, guys, there's lots of stuff around. So, what IS stuff, anyway?

Stuff seems to be rocks and trees and earth, Aruni said, but is really made up of a system of tiny building blocks too small to be seen!

Nobody paid much attention to this idea except other philosophers. After all, it was all purely theoretical and likely to stay so, because it could never be proved, one way or another, right? ...Or could it?

Fact Snack

In the past, history books were rather Euro-centric, but many developments are now being tracked further back in time to Asia. For example, some Chinese people worked out how to inoculate their children with viruses centuries before vaccines were developed in Europe. They ground up smallpox sores into powder, and fed it to their children. (Eww!)

Here, try some! You won't be SORE-ry!

In the first millennium BC, there was a growing crossover of ideas between the East and West, and the "what is stuff anyway?" discussion drifted over from India to a Mediterranean country called Greece, and into the mind of someone who took it further, about 400 years after Aruni lived.

A young man named Democritus had inherited money from his rich father and decided to spend it educating himself. He travelled to many countries, collected facts like modern people collect photographs, and then hired a professor to work with him so that their conversations would produce knowledge. It's lucky for us that he did, because a lot of the ideas that he and his teacher Leucippus came up with became important in science.

All that travelling, and my big discovery is at home.

Democritus was a funny guy who was known as a bit of a comedian. But he could also be serious when he wanted to be, and he felt that the Indian sage's idea was right. All stuff was made from a mysterious system of tiny, tiny, TINY building blocks which were very different from what we actually see. He reckoned it HAD to be that way, if you thought about it hard enough. When you cut things into smaller and smaller pieces, you would eventually have to get to a level where things cannot be cut any further, right? By definition, what's left would be "un-cuttable", which is *a-tomos* in Greek. Thus, all stuff must be made of uncuttables, or *a-tomos*.

Tater Toons

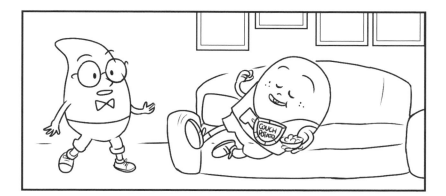

Tater Toons

Democritus thought about this a lot. During his meals, he popped something bitter into his mouth and decided that it must be made of sharp uncuttables. But his dessert was clearly made of smooth uncuttables.

He looked at the objects around him. Heavy, strong materials, such as iron, must be made of building blocks tightly hooked together, which is why you can't break a piece of metal. But soft substances, such as water, are surely made of loose particles which you can easily divide. They would be slippery *a-tomos*.

His great idea, unfortunately for him, would soon be scrapped and replaced by a different idea – by Aristotle, who was thought by many to be one of the smartest people who ever lived.

Aristotle was born many decades after Democritus, but also in Greece, so they may have overlapped with each other. But whether or not they met, Aristotle didn't support Democritus's view. He said that there were basic elements, such as earth, fire, water and air, and that when you broke them down into tinier pieces, everything was "continuous". What that meant was that an ocean of water could be reduced to a great many cups of water, which could be reduced to a great many drops of water, and so on. Even at tiny levels, water droplets were still water drops – just smaller.

There was much discussion among the elite about the really big questions of life at this time. People discussed the nature of reality ("what is stuff?") and related issues ("how should a person live?") around the world.

Are you intrigued by the row between Democritus and Aristotle? Scan the QR code on this page to go to a video that tells you more about how Aristotle's system came to dominate thinking for a long time.

Let's sC**ROOT**inise!

Something strange and wonderful happened to humanity in the period that stretches from Aruni to Aristotle, historians say. The great "intellectual traditions" of humanity evolved around the world at this time, from about 800 BC to about 400 BC.

Confucianism and Daoism developed in China, Hinduism and Buddhism in India, monotheism in the Middle East, and Socratic "intellectualism" (analytical thinking) in Greece.

Nobody knows why there was such a rush of long-lasting, world-changing ideas at this time – or whether there will be another period like it.

Aristotle's explanation (that big bits of water can be broken into small bits of water) was way easier to accept. So Democritus's idea of a world made of super-small invisible building blocks that don't look like the things they make was assigned to the bin.

And that's how things stood for not just centuries, but for about 2,000 years. If Democritus was looking down on earth from a cloud somewhere, he'd feel pretty depressed, that's for sure: a forgotten man with a forgotten idea. Awwww! But would it stay that way forever? Read on!

Chapter 3

A brief two millenniums later...

Once there was a doctor who was extremely proud of his nose. It was not particularly because of its size or shape, but because of its extraordinary smelling power.

Our story moves all the way to the 1600s, when a French doctor-professor named Johann Chrysostom Magnenus (let's just call him "Dr M") read about Democritus and believed the man had been onto something. The medical man wrote a book called *Democritus or Revival of the Atom* and set about measuring the size of the uncuttables by separating them and using his nose to locate a single *a-tomos*, or atom, by its smell. Dr M had a simple but brilliant plan. He lit a tiny lump of incense in an old, abandoned church. Then he explored the furthest corners of the inside of the building and waited for a single atom of the incense to reach him.

When he detected the distinctive smell, it meant that one atom of incense, at least, had reached his nostrils.

Then he sat down with pencil and paper and worked out things like the comparative volumes of the inside of the church and the inside of his nose.

The final figure he came up with for the estimated size of an atom was a tiny number with lots of zeroes after the decimal point, indicating that atoms were very, very small indeed.

Tater Toons

I read that noses can detect at least one trillion distinct smells, and half the pleasure of food comes not from the taste, but from the aroma.

Really? So, potato-mate-o, how would you feel if I moved the sofa to the kitchen?

Dr M's estimate was wrong by one zero. That may actually seem like quite a lot, if you think of the difference between 10 million and 100 million, for example. But it was impressively close for that time period. The difference between the smallest atom, helium, at 30 picometers, and the largest, caesium, at 300 picometers, is also one zero. Maybe Dr M's nose should now be listed as a key instrument in the history of science.

My calculation was off by one zero, so technically I got 'nothing' wrong.

The revival of interest in atoms sparked much discussion. The famous scientists of this period were divided. Michael Faraday said that the evidence for the existence of atoms did not reach his standards of proof. James Clark Maxwell, on the other hand, looked at the discussions on the topic and soon became convinced that there really was a strange and mysterious level of reality that looked very different from what we see around us.

Who would you talk to for more information on such a mysterious topic? How about going to... an alchemist?

Let's sC**ROOT**inise!

What image does the word "alchemist" summon in your head? Many people see wizards, witches or warlocks, working with strange potions in secret chambers.

In stories, alchemists are usually obsessed with turning ordinary metal into gold.

And in real life? Same thing! Alchemists didn't dress like wizards in storybooks, but did spend a lot of time with strange potions, and the transmutation (a fancy word for "changing") of cheap metal into gold was always the number one topic.

Alchemy was not considered odd or unscientific in those days. Isaac Newton, considered by many as one of the greatest scientists who ever lived, called himself an alchemist.

And the alchemist we are about to meet won the title "father of chemistry".

Now you'd probably imagine alchemists wore robes with stars on them and had names like "The Great Wizzo, Master of Magic".

But ours had a very plain name: Robert Boyle. He was a rather serious Irishman who once met Galileo Galilei on his travels, and was inspired to become a scientist – although that word had not yet been invented at that time, of course. For all we know, his friends may have called him Bob the Alchemist.

One of his first important jobs was to persuade the king to remove a law that made it illegal to try to create gold or silver through experiments. Transmutation must be achieved! In the end, our alchemist never managed to actually create gold, but he did make a lot of scientific breakthroughs.

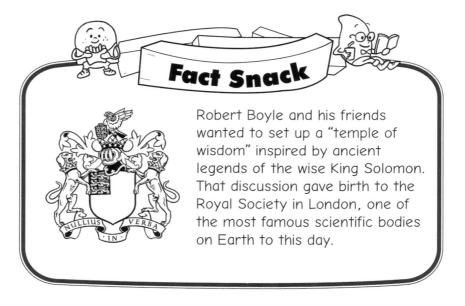

Fact Snack

Robert Boyle and his friends wanted to set up a "temple of wisdom" inspired by ancient legends of the wise King Solomon. That discussion gave birth to the Royal Society in London, one of the most famous scientific bodies on Earth to this day.

One of Boyle's insights was to realise that all objects were made of two things: the relatively big visible structure and the very small invisible building blocks. You could even keep the structure of an object while swapping out the blocks for different ones, he believed. So trees are made of wood, but it would be possible to have a tree made of stone, for example.

That sounds weird, right? But the idea turned out to be right. Years later, when scientists understood fossilisation, it was clear that Bob the Alchemist had been bang on target. His theory explains why dinosaur fossils look like bones but are actually made of rock, and why lumps of coal sometimes look like pieces of wood.

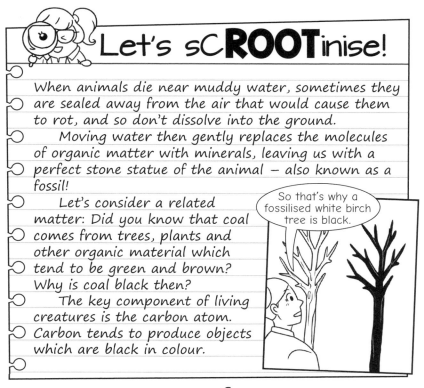

Let's sC**ROOT**inise!

When animals die near muddy water, sometimes they are sealed away from the air that would cause them to rot, and so don't dissolve into the ground.

Moving water then gently replaces the molecules of organic matter with minerals, leaving us with a perfect stone statue of the animal — also known as a fossil!

Let's consider a related matter: Did you know that coal comes from trees, plants and other organic material which tend to be green and brown? Why is coal black then?

The key component of living creatures is the carbon atom. Carbon tends to produce objects which are black in colour.

So that's why a fossilised white birch tree is black.

If you want to visualise exactly how a dinosaur turns into a fossil, scan this QR code to see how this happens in an animation by the Natural History Museum in London.

In the following century, the 1700s, a shy man called Henry Cavendish got into the habit of spending a lot of time in his work room doing experiments so he wouldn't have to go out and meet people. One of his ideas was that even air was made up of atoms and that there were different types of air, made up of different atoms. People already knew that oxygen was an important element of air, but were there others?

Whoa!

Henry Cavendish put some metal in a test tube and poured acid on it, and it fizzed into gas. Oddly, this new type of air could be set on fire! And even more bizarrely, when he lit it with a match or a candle, there was a flash of fire: the air disappeared and water was left behind! He worked out that the burnable air (which was later given the name hydrogen) produced water when it was mixed with oxygen.

Henry Cavendish even worked out the proportions. If atoms did exist, you would take two atoms of hydrogen and add one atom of oxygen, and the result would be one molecule of water.

Fact Snack

Today, scientists refer to water as H_2O, which of course is short for "two hydrogen atoms plus one atom of oxygen". Shy Henry may have hated the idea of actually speaking to humans, but he had managed to get himself talked about centuries later.

When we three get together, our hands magically feel wet!

Chapter 4

Dancing zombie plant seeds

One day, a botanist (a plant expert) went to see an optician. Instead of a pair of glasses, he asked the man to make him a microscope so that he could look more closely at his beloved flowers.

The botanist hurried home and put some tiny grains of pollen (the powdery stuff inside flowers that sticks to the legs of bees) into some water and looked at it through the microscope. He was astonished to find that the tiny dust-like particles were moving around, and even going on long walks. This made no sense – how could plant seeds go for walks, like animals?

Fact Snack

Plants never grow into animals and animals never become plants, but there is one plant that dances to music, just like animals. The Dancing Plant, scientific name *Desmodium gyrans*, gently twirls its long thin leaves if you play music to it. Watch it dance by scanning the QR code in this box.

The botanist, Robert Brown, repeated the experiment with pollen from a plant that he knew had been dead for more than 20 years. Again, he found the pollen grains moving by themselves, despite being definitely deceased. This was getting spooky!

He then went and got a plant that had been preserved, dead, for more than 100 years. That plant's long-dead pollen did the same thing, scurrying about randomly on long walks. Zombie plant seeds!

Robert Brown wrote an essay about it and the scientific community of that period, the early 1800s, was intrigued. Why did the botanist's tiny dead flakes of pollen dust come to life and go for rambling walks, wading through little pools of water? It was the random paths that the flakes took that really puzzled people.

Elsewhere in the UK, also in the early 1800s, a chemist named John Dalton experimented with mixed gases and powdered metals, and realised that there was something very odd about his results.

The proportions of each substance were suspiciously neat. As he made new mixtures out of different elements, he ended up with a simple answer: one compound had exactly twice as much of a certain element as another compound – not seven-and-a-bit, or eight and thirteen-fourteenths, or x2.62746, but exactly twice as much. Repeated experiments with different substances gave him the same results. What could it mean?

Suddenly, it clicked. He realised that the neat results revealed an underlying truth: his seemingly complex compounds were actually made of simple combinations of atoms. The theory of atoms was true!

Fact Snack

At this stage, the atomists decided that they knew what atoms looked like and drew them as small, solid ball-shaped things. This became known as the "billiard balls model" of the atom.

Remember, junior, life is full of traps, especially in table-corners.

A British doctor named Richard Laming had a hobby of trying to work out how electricity worked in his spare time. In those days, people generally didn't have electricity in their homes, so it was not something familiar. But they saw electricity in lightning strikes, and some knew about static electricity and magnetism. And who could blame them? It was a challenge trying to study something you only see for half a second every few months!

Fact Snack

Although people have only had electricity in their homes for a few generations, the oldest known written reference to electrical activity may be in China's 2,400-year-old *Book of the Devil Valley Master*, which mentions magnetism. "The lodestone makes iron come," the author wrote. (Lodestone is an old word for a magnetic rock.)

Are you READY TO ROCK?

By 1838, scientists had worked out that electric charge came from a flow of atoms. Dr Laming suggested that perhaps atoms were little round things that had elements inside them which generated energy. He imagined them to contain a middle part surrounded by shells. Perhaps the pieces operated as a machine to create electricity?

His ideas didn't get much reaction, perhaps because he did not express them well or with good enough experimental data. Still, with Dr Laming and others speculating about what might be inside atoms, an idea started to grow that the uncuttables might not be able to live up to their name. Perhaps you *could* cut them!

In 1853, a teenage boy from Russia spent months in the hospital. A doctor said, "This one will never recover." But Dmitri Mendeleev took it as a challenge and fought his way back to health.

As an adult, he became a science teacher and had to teach a course in chemistry. But he couldn't find a good textbook, so he decided to write one himself. Where to start?

Sitting at his desk, Mendeleev decided that he needed to put all the known elements of the world into logical order so that he could write the contents page, the list of chapters.

To do that, he had to think about what was known about each element at the time, from gases like hydrogen and helium, to metals like iron and gold.

Fact Snack

I'm not dead, so that's a win.

Mendeleev saw himself as a science investigator. He went to meetings of people who claimed to have psychic powers to see if such things were real (he decided that a lot of them weren't). He once flew solo in a hot air balloon to investigate whether there was a vacuum instead of air at high altitudes.

To write his chapter list, Mendeleev wrote down everything he knew about every known element and organised them in ways that made sense to him. He was fascinated to see that elements weren't random, but fell into an intelligent pattern.

He continued to work on it, and – POW! – he had created history. The list was the basis of a chart that is so important that it can now be found in every school: the Periodic Table, which is a sort of family tree for elements.

By doing this job so well, he serendipitously (that means "by lucky accident") achieved two unexpected bonuses. First, gaps in his chart predicted the existence of substances before they were actually discovered, so people could go look for them. Second, the way that elements were related to each other gave scientists information about which molecules were made of which atoms and what atoms might have inside them.

This might have been the first time that the really special part of a book was not the contents, but the contents page!

PERIODIC TABLE OF ELEMENTS

H															Pub C hem		He
Li	Be					H	Symbol						B	C	N	O	F	Ne
Na	Mg												Al	Si	P	S	Cl	Ar
K	Ca	Sc	Ti	V	Cr	Mn	Fe	Co	Ni	Cu	Zn	Ga	Ge	As	Se	Br	Kr
Rb	Sr	Y	Zr	Nb	Mo	Tc	Ru	Rh	Pd	Ag	Cd	In	Sn	Sb	Te	I	Xe
Cs	Ba		Hf	Ta	W	Re	Os	Ir	Pt	Au	Hg	Tl	Pb	Bi	Po	At	Rn
Fr	Ra		Rf	Db	Sg	Bh	Hs	Mt	Ds	Rg	Cn	Nh	Fl	Mc	Lv	Ts	Og
			La	Ce	Pr	Nd	Pm	Sm	Eu	Gd	Tb	Dy	Ho	Er	Tm	Yb	Lu
			Ac	Th	Pa	U	Np	Pu	Am	Cm	Bk	Cf	Es	Fm	Md	No	Lr

Find out more about Mendeleev's story and the periodic table by scanning the QR code on this page. If you want to memorise the whole of the periodic table, there's actually a funny song that helps you do just that!

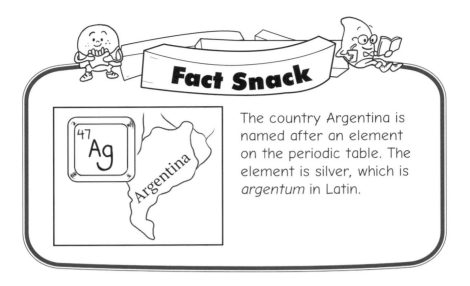

Fact Snack

The country Argentina is named after an element on the periodic table. The element is silver, which is *argentum* in Latin.

We have now reached the late 1800s, when a man named Joseph John Thomson (whom everyone called J.J.) was looking at a piece of equipment on his desk that created cathode rays. In front of him was a glass tube containing electrodes in a vacuum. When he put an electric charge across the electrodes, a glow of light appeared on the glass.

Because he had done his physics homework, he knew that the glow was caused by tiny particles of light with a negative electrical charge landing on the glass.

But here's the important bit: J.J. realised that electrical charges could be measured. He did that and found that the number known as the "mass-to-charge ratio" was 1,800 times smaller than that of a hydrogen atom. So the little glowing things were very, very little indeed – smaller than the smallest known thing.

What were these tiny things?

They surely came from inside atoms... so now we had proof! Uncuttables weren't solid blocks of something after all. Aha!

Let's sC**ROOT**inise!

John Dalton's billiard ball model of the atom was gently pushed off the table. A new model was needed.

After reading Thomson's work, scientists re-drew the atom as a sort of solid-ish globe studded on the inside with tiny dots – the little electrical things that he had found.

This was given the nickname "the plum pudding model", named after a type of sweet, rich British dessert containing raisins.

I'll write up this huge discovery in the science journals ... after dessert.

J.J. Thomson accepted the nickname of "plum pudding" for the new design of the atom model. But he made sure that scientists knew that in his theory, the new little particles moved all the time. In contrast, raisins don't crawl about, unless there is something very wrong indeed with your pudding!

Still, the community decided to keep the word "atom", even if it did turn out to be cuttable. But they needed a name for the tiny particles.

Let's sC**ROOT**inise!

An Irish physicist named George Johnston Stoney suggested the word "Electrolion" in 1881 for the super-small particles. Just think of the wonderful images of tiny lions that word would have conjured up.

But other scientists ruled it out and the new sub-atomic particle was eventually named the Electron, which means "amber" in Greek.

One of the earliest discoveries of electricity was when people 2,000 years ago noticed that when you rubbed fur against amber, a transparent orange stone, you produced static electricity.

Chapter 5

Einstein meets the atom

Now we have reached the 1900s, when most scientists had come to believe in atoms. We had names for some atoms, and even for one item which seemed to hide inside them: the electron.

It's now time to meet a very clever young clerk at a patent office in Switzerland. His name was Albert Einstein, and he was 26. He had gotten into the habit of reading science journals for fun, not something most people would do. But he had liked physics at school.

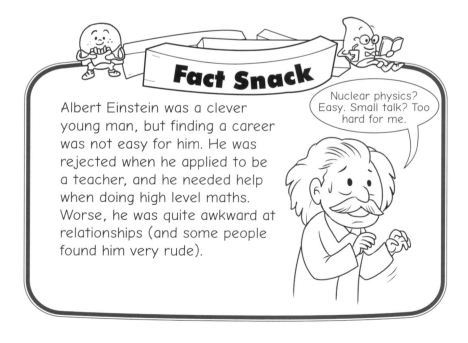

Fact Snack

Albert Einstein was a clever young man, but finding a career was not easy for him. He was rejected when he applied to be a teacher, and he needed help when doing high level maths. Worse, he was quite awkward at relationships (and some people found him very rude).

Nuclear physics? Easy. Small talk? Too hard for me.

One day, Albert Einstein thought about the puzzle of Robert Brown's self-propelled pollen grains (the "zombie seeds" from earlier) and the more recent work on atoms, and he realised what the answer to the mystery was.

Pollen grains were tiny and lightweight but visible to the human eye. Atoms, on the other hand, were tiny and lightweight but NOT visible. The pollen grains weren't running around because they were alive, they were moving only because invisible atoms were active in the water, leading them in a dance.

Other people had already speculated about whether atoms were involved, but Einstein explained it all with clear mathematics and explanations to back up his argument. This made it conclusive. The mystery of the dancing zombie plant dust had been solved.

Fact Snack

In 1905, Albert Einstein had five essays (including the one about the zombie pollen mystery) published in science journals and all were considered important breakthroughs. Some people called it Einstein's "miracle year".

My discoverer, Albert, had a string of hits this year.

A few years later, one of J.J. Thomson's students decided to stay in scientific research after finishing university and followed the trail laid down by his teacher, creator of the yummy-sounding plum pudding model of the atom.

Student Ernest Rutherford had been born on a farm in New Zealand, but had decided he would travel anywhere in the world where he could get a good education in the things that interested him.

Being a scientist sounds fun, but the truth is that most research work is very boring. For several years, he and his colleagues set up their lab equipment so that they could fire tiny particles through slightly larger particles and write down what happened.

This could give them some information about what was inside an atom. Would the "bullets" move through the "pudding" quickly or slowly? Would some bump into the "raisins" and be slowed down further or moved slightly off track?

What actually happened was totally unexpected. Most of the particles flew straight through but a small number, about one in 8,000, hit something tiny and hard and bounced back. He was shocked. Now this must be a clue about what was inside! What could it mean?

Let's sCROOTinise!

Ernest Rutherford had tried to build experimental evidence to add details to his teacher's discovery of the "plum pudding model" of the atom — but the results demolished it.

Oh bother! The pudding model's gone! What will we serve at the annual science party?

> The findings showed that atoms were mostly empty except for something very tiny but rather strong at the centre.
> This mysterious blob was given the name "the nucleus". A new branch of scientific study opened up: nuclear physics, which is what you are studying now.
> Today, when we think of the word "nuclear", we picture big things like power plants and intercontinental missiles.
> But they are named after something very small: the dot in the middle of each atom.

In the following years, scientists worked out in detail what an atom was. It was a globe-shaped object with a nucleus in the middle of it, just as Dr Richard Laming had suggested.

The atom itself contained tiny elements they called subatomic particles. The most important of these seemed to be the electron.

But there were other subatomic elements found too, although they were not as small as the electron. It was discovered that the nucleus was made up of two types of subatomic particles, which were called protons and neutrons.

And scientists also worked out the key difference between different atoms. It was how many protons and/or neutrons could be found in the nucleus. So a hydrogen atom had one proton and no neutrons. A helium atom had two protons and either one or two neutrons. And so on.

The early atomists would have been amazed at the size and complexity of the atoms we have discovered today. For example, there's an important one called Uranium-235, which has 143 neutrons and 92 protons in its centre, and 92 electrons outside the nucleus. It's a biggie!

Let's sCROOTinise!

In the early 1900s, scientists realised it was time for a new picture of the atom. The billiard ball model had gone, and now the plum pudding model had been scrapped.

The new diagram became known as the planetary system model. That's because it looked a bit like a solar system — the nucleus was the sun and the electrons randomly orbiting it were the planets.

Finally, we had the right answer! The new diagram was so detailed that it wouldn't have to be changed again. Or so it seemed. But we've heard that one before, right?

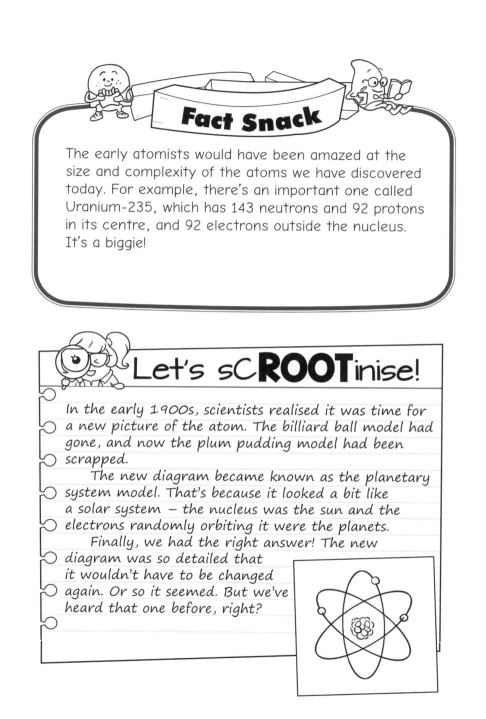

One day, Ernest Rutherford was working with a colleague named Frederick Soddy in a laboratory on strange substances that seemed to give off invisible rays of energy – what we now call radioactivity, as discovered by Marie Curie.

They wondered what caused this to happen.

Suddenly, they realised that radioactivity was caused by the transmutation of elements! Something was happening inside the atoms which was causing one substance to be transformed into another substance, just as the alchemists had predicted centuries ago. So it WAS possible after all!

Soddy yelled, "Rutherford, this is transmutation! The thorium is disintegrating and transmuting itself into argon gas!"

Rutherford replied, "For Mike's sake, Soddy, don't call it transmutation. They'll have our heads off as

Oh dear... Have we become wizards?!

alchemists!" He was worried that other scientists would picture them as the sort of wizards who would try to turn cheap metal into gold.

But that didn't happen. The other physicists realised that Rutherford and Soddy were making important discoveries about stuff. Stuff could become other stuff, as the wizards and alchemists had predicted centuries ago. We were finally getting some interesting answers to Aruni's observation.

Does this mean that if you became a scientist, you can turn a piece of cheap metal, like an empty drink can, into gold?

Yes, you can — in theory. But probably not in practice.

That's because while it is possible to change the elements outside the nucleus using chemical reactions (which is what Rutherford and Soddy did), making gold is trickier. To make gold, you'd have to change the elements INSIDE the nucleus, which is very difficult.

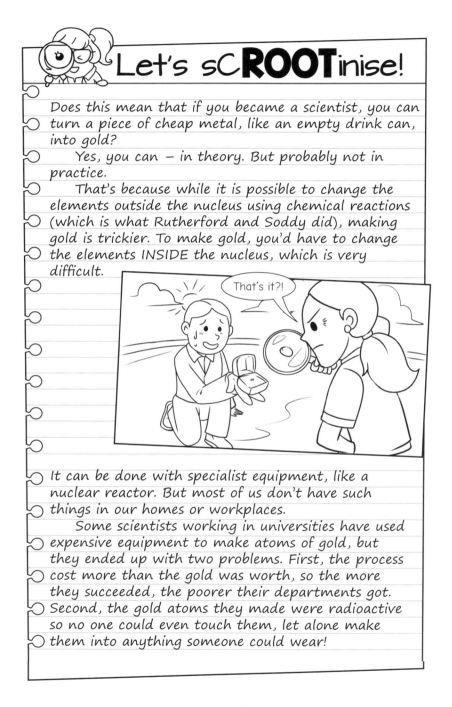

It can be done with specialist equipment, like a nuclear reactor. But most of us don't have such things in our homes or workplaces.

Some scientists working in universities have used expensive equipment to make atoms of gold, but they ended up with two problems. First, the process cost more than the gold was worth, so the more they succeeded, the poorer their departments got. Second, the gold atoms they made were radioactive so no one could even touch them, let alone make them into anything someone could wear!

Chapter 6

A world-shaking discovery

An important new character enters our story in this section, which focuses on the first half of the 1900s. He was a Danish man named Niels Bohr. He and his colleagues investigated the nature of atoms and they put the Aruni/Democritus theory right back on top. They agreed that the atom could be defined as the smallest unit into which stuff can be divided without interfering with it. So even though you can cut atoms, they still counted as the basic building blocks of matter, the starting point of everything.

Now it was just a matter of sorting out the different types of atoms and making charts. Everything seemed settled. The rest of the work on atoms, some people thought, would be very easy, straightforward and predictable.

Until Niels Bohr started digging deeper.

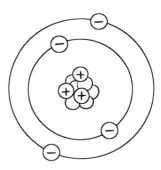

Now, Niels Bohr was a details sort of guy and the more he studied, the more he saw things that didn't quite fit. Experiments revealed that electrons do not travel around the nucleus in random orbits as Rutherford thought. They seemed to travel at fixed distances from the nucleus.

But this was the weird bit. If you added energy to an atom, the electron would instantly disappear and then materialise at a higher orbit, further away from the centre, and if you extracted energy from an electron, it would disappear to materialise in a lower orbit.

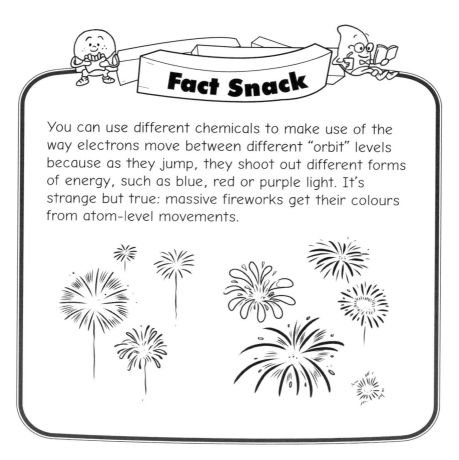

Fact Snack

You can use different chemicals to make use of the way electrons move between different "orbit" levels because as they jump, they shoot out different forms of energy, such as blue, red or purple light. It's strange but true: massive fireworks get their colours from atom-level movements.

As Bohr continued to study atoms, he realised that it was the actual way electrons jumped that was extraordinary. In the real world, the only way to get from A to B was to move through the space between. But that wasn't happening. The electrons just disappeared from one space and appeared in another.

This odd ability of subatomic particles became known as the "quantum leap".

Let's scROOTinise!

It's a bit strange that in the modern English idiom, the word "quantum leap" is used to refer to a very large jump: either an actual literal leap from one spot to another, or used as a metaphor for a move between two widely distanced ideas.

In fact, the term originally described the smallest movement you could possible imagine — a tiny displacement inside an atom.

Even more bizarrely, a real quantum leap wasn't a leap at all. The whole issue was that the electron didn't jump or leap but transported itself in a way that is impossible according to the rules of this reality.

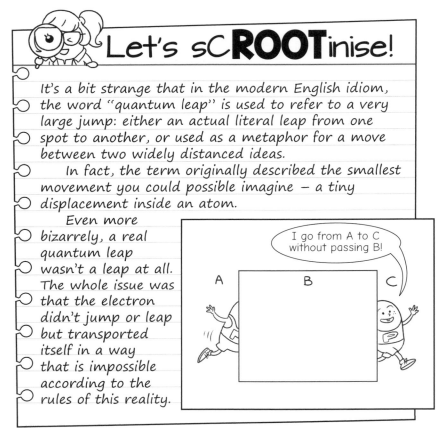

I go from A to C without passing B!

A   B   C

Fact Snack

A particle is a thing. But a wave, in scientific terms, is not a thing, but a way that things move. How can something be both a thing and not a thing? Scientists saw this as a clue that the basic matter that made up all "stuff" was more intriguing than it seemed.

Many people at that time thought there must be something wrong with the work of Niels Bohr and his colleagues. What they were saying about atoms was so illogical that Albert Einstein, whom many people think of as the archetypal scientific thinker, decided that the findings must be either wrong, or, at the very least, missing something important.

Have you ever wondered how the argument between Einstein and Bohr was like? It seems that many people have. So much so that National Geographic made a live-action mini-movie of it (using actors to play the great scientists, of course). Scan the QR code to watch that video.

But it was also known that Niels Bohr and his colleagues were the best sort of scientists: careful people who looked at evidence intelligently. Many people felt confident that these bizarre oddities would soon be resolved.

Instead, the mystery deepened. [Cue more dramatic music!]

Fact Snack

As a university student, Niels Bohr became known for causing explosions in the chemistry lab and was said to have destroyed a record amount of glass. So it was good that he became a theoretical physicist, which meant he looked at other people's data and worked out what it meant – but didn't have to spend time in labs himself.

Sorry about your lab. I'll make it up to you with some history-making science discoveries.

Under the investigations of Bohr and his colleagues, the atom became increasingly illogical. The scientists reported that "looking" at an atom seemed to bring it into existence. Before that, it was just a potential atom. (We put "looking" in quotation marks, because of course we can't look at atoms in the normal way with our eyes. Instead, we use special machines to detect their presence.)

What's more, atoms seem to behave differently if they were being watched, the data showed!

Tater Toons

In 1925, a young physicist called Werner Heisenberg (say it: Ver-na Hi-zen-burg) looked at a pile of data and tried to find a way to work out where a particle was and where it was going. Should be easy enough, right?

But it wasn't. When Heisenberg worked out exactly where the particle was, he found the details of its speed and direction were impossible to pin down. So he tried it the other way. He worked out the particle's precise speed and direction. But then he found he couldn't work out exactly where the particle was.

At first, it seemed like some sort of irritating mistake in his pages of maths equations. But gradually he realised that he had stumbled upon a secret of the universe.

There is something built into the bedrock of reality, which means you can never uncover the full truth about particles. It was as if atoms weren't objects at all. They were just clues. They were literally just ideas and even then, they were not full concepts, but just hints at the possible existence of stuff. His discovery became known as "The Uncertainty Principle".

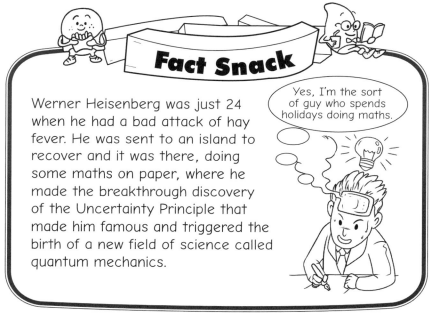

Fact Snack

Werner Heisenberg was just 24 when he had a bad attack of hay fever. He was sent to an island to recover and it was there, doing some maths on paper, where he made the breakthrough discovery of the Uncertainty Principle that made him famous and triggered the birth of a new field of science called quantum mechanics.

Yes, I'm the sort of guy who spends holidays doing maths.

Now, Albert Einstein, who was already fed up with the quantum physicists, decided that this seemed just a bit too weird. He said that if things weren't in a particular place at a particular time and didn't exist until a person randomly chose to look at them, it would be as if God had built a game of dice into the basic elements of reality.

But other scientists said that randomness was a good thing. Without it, the universe would be just like a big machine doing everything automatically, robotically and predictably. It would also mean that there would be no such thing as free will and life would be very boring since we would have no real choices to make.

It was the randomness and unpredictability built into every atom that made life interesting, they said.

The work of the young German scientist meant that we had to again throw away, or at least revise, our diagram of the atom.

Out went the "planetary model" of the atom, in which a dot in the middle was surrounded by neat rows of circles.

In came a new model in which we had a nucleus at the middle, and around it, a fuzzy general area where the electrons would PROBABLY be found. Scientists described it as "the cloud of probability".

You will have noticed that Einstein was doing a lot of complaining in those days. He had become the undisputed king of "regular" science but the atomists with their sub-atomic particles were painting a different image of the world.

Their atoms, he complained, showed "spooky actions at a distance", or in other words, that things done in one place caused reactions at a different place. This was the sort of thing you saw in stories of magic, wizards and witches, but not in real life, and especially not in the serious world of science. Many of the curious discoveries about subatomic particles were grouped under the term "quantum weirdness".

Chapter 7

The dots that could power a city

Ready for everything to go BOOM? Good. It's explosion time! Now we get to the secret of the tremendous energy inside atoms. Where is it hidden? It's not in the nucleus or the electrons whizzing around, so you might be able to guess where it is. (And we told you earlier! Were you paying attention?)

Yes. It's in the glue that holds it all together. This "glue" is not sticky stuff that you get in your school stationery box. Instead, it's an invisible force that comes in several "flavours". Think of it as the binding energy that holds the system in place. Break it, and the energy from the tiny system is released.

Tater Toons

Let's release some energy! How do we do that? All we need to do is spend a few years and a lot of money to build a machine that can fire a neutron at the right speed at the centre of the atom. It hits the nucleus, which then splits into two pieces, releasing a burst of energy.

Fact Snack

Just tell me it's not green in colour...

Did you know that there is an element called Krypton? No, it didn't take its name from superhero comics or movies. It is an element discovered by chemists in 1898. When you split an atom of Uranium-235, it breaks into two elements: an atom of Barium and an atom of Krypton.

Of course, an individual atom is a very, very, very small thing and the energy produced from splitting one won't be large, but it's what happens next that is interesting. Atoms don't sit on a shelf by themselves. They come in very large numbers, closely packed together. When you split one (scientists say "when you achieve nuclear fission"), other neutrons shoot out and hit the nuclei of the atoms around the first one. Those atoms also split in two, more neutrons shoot out, and those hit other atoms.

This is what is called a chain reaction. All this takes place in a very short space of time – just fractions of a second. The result is that a huge amount of energy can be released from a tiny object. And when we say huge, we mean very large indeed, like the heat of the sun, close-up.

Fact Snack

The Voyager space probe, launched in the 1970s, has been successfully powered by nuclear reactions for decades. An atom called plutonium decays naturally and produces heat energy without the need for atom-splitting.

If you want to create energy, which atom should be used? Well, one of the curious things about atoms is that small is stronger than big. But small simple atoms are much harder to split than bigger ones.

So people who want to create this type of energy tend to go for larger atoms. Experiments showed that an atom called Uranium-235 (remember, we said it was extra-large?) worked best for this process.

The world was on the edge of war in the late 1930s. In 1938, the first atom was split. Those were tense times. Scientists on all sides were becoming aware that nuclear physics could be used, in theory, to create a bomb more powerful than anyone had ever seen before. Yeah, the smallest thing in the world is also the most dangerous thing in the world – weird, right?

Albert Einstein wrote a famous letter to US President Franklin Roosevelt warning him that terrible things could happen if Adolf Hitler in Germany made "atomic" bombs.

There was soon a huge team of people, about 200,000 of them, working on the project in the United States. Quite a few of the scientists on the project were from Germany. The atomic bomb was eventually assembled and then tested in a desert in a place called New Mexico.

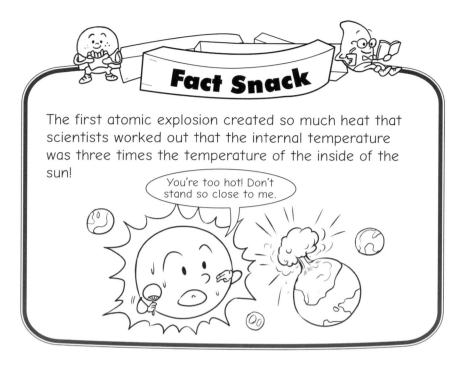

Fact Snack

The first atomic explosion created so much heat that scientists worked out that the internal temperature was three times the temperature of the inside of the sun!

Later, atom bombs were dropped on two cities in Japan. It is believed that more than 135,000 people were killed in Hiroshima and another 70,000 in Nagasaki. Many died instantly, while others died over the following months and years.

The decision to use the bombs was very controversial and remains so today. American leaders argued that more lives would have been lost if they hadn't dropped the bombs. But the Japanese argued that although they technically hadn't surrendered, it was obvious to everyone that their army had been defeated by that time. So why did so many civilians have to die horrible deaths?

Some people argue about whether nuclear power plants or solar power systems are the best choice for providing clean energy. From a scientist's point of view, they are the exact same thing! The sun is a natural nuclear power plant, a safe distance away.

Nuclear energy looks like a dream come true – it's all around us and doesn't cost anything. And better still, it does not contribute much to global warming. But there are downsides. The waste produced by the process is dangerous and must be thrown far away from human beings.

And it's a long-term challenge. If your clothes or toys become radioactive, they may stay that way for thousands of years.

Let's sC**ROOT**inise!

In recent centuries, the field of science was dominated by men, but there have been plenty of women making huge contributions. Einstein started his journey into science as a young man with long conversations with his first wife Mileva, who was also a student of theoretical physics.

Another big contributor to progress during this time was a brilliant mathematician named Emmy Noether, who was often the only female sitting among large groups of young men at lectures in those days. There were also non-European people involved in the atomic breakthroughs, too, like Wu Chien-Shiung from China.

> Guys hog the headlines, but there are plenty of women playing key roles.

Among the experimental scientists providing evidence for the advances in atom studies being made in the first half of the 1900s, one of the most important was Marie Curie. She discovered radium, a substance that emitted large amounts of radioactivity, way back in 1898.

Our story has come a long way from Democritus, 2,400 years ago, via people like Dalton and Rutherford, all the way to the findings of Heisenberg. If you want a useful video recap of the story so far, scan this QR code.

Chapter 8

Antimatter in the particle zoo

More and more particles were found during the middle period of the 1900s. By the beginning of the 1960s, people started to talk about the "particle zoo" as if it was a massive gathering of different looking creatures. There were big atoms, small atoms and some with strange superpowers.

Fact Snack

Particles called muons are born in the upper atmosphere and only survive for a brief moment – certainly not long enough for them to make the journey all the way to earth. So scientists were puzzled to find some at ground level. How did they get here before disappearing? They discovered that muons move so fast that they do some time travelling on the way!

I'm going to do some time travelling and spend my last moments on a beach down there.

The particle zoo seemed totally chaotic and random. But things rarely are, right? An American scientist named Murray Gell-Mann guessed that there must be some sort of logical system behind this (just like Mendeleev realised when looking at elements almost 100 years earlier). Science, like mathematics, is full of hidden patterns that turn out to be elegant and balanced.

Is the pattern stripes, checks or floral?

Gell-Mann worked out that if you mapped out all the different types of atomic or subatomic particles, you would eventually get a pattern that was symmetrical in shape. He drew this out and the resulting diagram led him to make some guesses to fill in the missing bits (just like Mendeleev had).

Perhaps the most surprising result of this work was the implied locations of some of the new particles. You remember that the nucleus is the hard bit in the middle of each atom, containing two types of subatomic particles, protons and neutrons? Gell-Mann's symmetrical chart showed that you needed MORE subatomic particles and that they would be found in the nucleus, INSIDE the protons and neutrons. Each would contain three smaller elements, all slightly different.

Fact Snack

Most scientists who make up names for things use Greek and Latin. But Gell-Mann broke the tradition calling the new tiny particles "quarks" (a made-up word from a novel), which he pronounced "kworks", just because he liked the sound and thought it suited the mysterious tiny things!

Quarks!

Other scientists realised that Gell-Mann's symmetrical model made sense and started doing experiments to find the items he said should exist. It took a few years, but by 1968, the quarks had been found.

As predicted, there were three inside each proton and three inside each neutron. This goes to show how theoretical physicists, who do the sitting and thinking, are just as important as experimental scientists, who spend their time in labs with test tubes.

Fact Snack

The new particles were also announced with non-traditional vocabulary. Scientists announced to the world that they had found six "flavours" of quarks, which they called up, down, charm, strange, top and bottom.

Tater Toons

That's not a zoo! There's nothing there!

It's a particle zoo. It's full of interesting particles.

The really annoying thing is that, technically, he's right.

In the last few decades of the 1900s, we learnt a lot about the rule of atoms in the history of everything. And symmetry studies taught us that since matter exists, so does antimatter.

Just after the Big Bang, 13.8 billion years ago, there were lots of tiny chemical reactions and these gave birth to atoms in the shape of matter and antimatter. Each of these met, cancelled out the other, and disappeared.

But, lucky for us, there was a one-in-a-billion imbalance. This meant that for every billion annihilations, a single particle of matter was left over. After a very, very, very, VERY long time, there were enough particles of matter to make a universe.

So here we are.

Let's sC**ROOT**inise!

Strange but true: you don't need a huge laboratory to make antimatter.

Bananas make antimatter. This is because they contain an atom called Potassium-40. This gently decays, occasionally emitting the antimatter version of electrons, which are called positrons.

But you don't need to be afraid to approach the fruit bowl at home. Banana-emitted positrons tend to disappear rapidly without triggering antimatter chain reactions, which destroy the planet. Phew! (So no shooting antimatter out of banana guns – sorry!)

Fact Snack

Human bodies also contain Potassium-40, so you can tell your friends that your body is an antimatter machine!

In science fiction books and movies, antimatter is often used as a weapon, but scientists say that in real life, that is one of the less likely uses for the stuff. You need large, heavy equipment (and LOADS of money) to make the stuff, so it's hard to build an actual portable antimatter gun.

But the real uses of antimatter are really interesting.

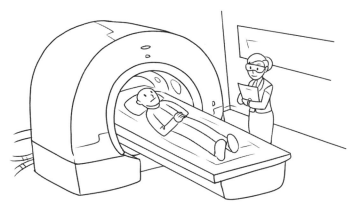

Have you ever visited a hospital? Then you may have been near a powerful antimatter machine.

Hospitals often do tests called PET scans. This stands for "positron emission tomography". Positrons are a type of antimatter, and are injected into people's bloodstreams before a PET scan. They produce gamma rays, which can be detected and used to create accurate pictures of the inside of people's bodies.

Let's sC**ROOT**inise!

Here are four amazing things about antimatter:

1) Scientists at CERN, the world's biggest particle physics lab, are studying the possible anti-gravity properties of antimatter. Imagine if they could be harnessed for useful purposes, such as making shoes that give you the power to fly!

I'm saving a fortune on air tickets.

2) Some scientists think that antimatter particles are normal particles that live backwards in time. If only particles could talk, we could learn about our future (which, of course, would be their past) from them.

3) Antimatter is the world's most expensive stuff. Because it is so hard to make, it costs at least US$25 billion a gram, and some say much more. Suddenly, gold and diamonds don't sound so expensive.

4) If you could store large amounts of antimatter, you could use it to power spacecraft — and you could do interplanetary or even interstellar flights.

Tater Toons

Chipping in: Today's scientists at work

Atoms are small, which makes them good for making very small things.

For example, Dr Jun Rui, a scientist at the Max-Planck Institute in Germany, has made the thinnest and lightest mirror in the world.

"It isn't a regular mirror but a quantum one," says the China-born scientist.

His mirror is soooo tiny that it is pretty much invisible, so you can't see your face in it. But it does capture light and reflect it, so it does count as a mirror.

Just how small is it? "It is seven micrometres in diameter," Dr Rui says, "and 10 nanometres in thickness." A micrometre is one millionth of a metre and a nanometre is one billionth of a metre. So the mirror is much, much smaller than the full stop at the end of this sentence.

Whoa, that is one BIG full stop. Or am I just tiny?

But here's what's interesting. As you have learnt in this book, things at a super-small level don't behave like "normal" objects.

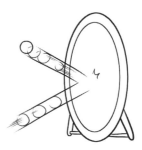

"What excites us most is that the photons that strike our mirror interact with the atoms that are hit," Dr Rui told reporters.

So the light particles don't just bounce back, but react with the mirror itself. What can you do with it? He's not sure yet.

In fact, that's a good question – what use is a mirror that's so small that you can't see your face in it?

The quantum mirror is not for people to use to look at themselves. It's for use in quantum computers and in microchips, to make them work better.

Dr Rui started his science education at the University of Science & Technology of China, which is in Hefei, Anhui province, not far from Shanghai. He was a physics student, so he had to study the people mentioned in this book, including Max Planck, who came up with the word "quantum".

After doing a doctorate in China, Dr Rui became a visiting scholar in a place called Heidelberg in Germany.

He now works in that country at an institute named after the man whose work he had to study as a young student many years earlier. Talk about coming full circle!

Chapter 9

Atoms everywhere!

Duck! There's a particle coming from outer space and it is aimed right at your body. In fact, it's going to hit you directly in a few seconds. Three... two... one... BANG! A perfect shot. Got you in the middle of your head.

That's not a joke. There really are particles coming from space that are making direct hits on you all the time. Lots of them are hitting you right now as you read this book.

We call them neutrinos, but they don't hurt. They are very strange, almost ghostlike objects, floating through walls and people as if they weren't there at all.

More than a trillion neutrinos pass through your body every second. That's because huge numbers of them are raining down on earth from the sun and from elsewhere in the galaxy all the time.

Get out the spare airbed, a trillion of us are visiting.

Neutrinos can even pass right through a planet, drifting effortlessly through the earth's molten metal core. They are yet another subatomic particle that behaves as if they belong to a reality separate from ours. They are so delicate that you need big, powerful detector machines that can be kept separate from everything else that's moving or buzzing or falling. For that reason, scientists usually build neutrino detecting machines in deep underground chambers.

How do you spot neutrinos, since you can't see them, hear them, smell them or feel them? They can be detected very, very occasionally in water. The vast majority of them fly through solid objects, including seas, lakes and swimming pools. But every ten millionth trillionth travelling neutrino will hit a water molecule and make a tiny flash that a machine can detect.

So we build huge water tanks underground, surrounded by neutrino detectors. The ground stops other particles getting to the tanks, making it easier for the machines to detect neutrinos.

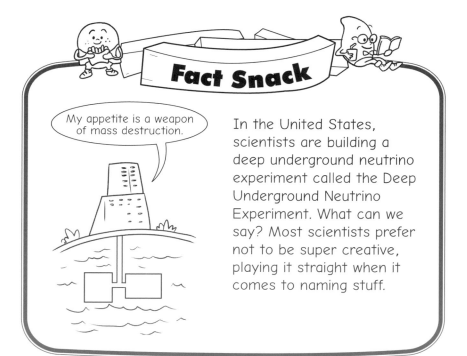

Fact Snack

My appetite is a weapon of mass destruction.

In the United States, scientists are building a deep underground neutrino experiment called the Deep Underground Neutrino Experiment. What can we say? Most scientists prefer not to be super creative, playing it straight when it comes to naming stuff.

Neutrinos show that we are still finding out new extraordinary things about atoms today. And much of what we learn really makes you think. For example, some particles, like neutrinos, have very little mass or no mass at all.

Mass is like weight, but slightly different – it is a measure of "how much stuff" there is in an object. So, think about it: if an object has ZERO stuff, how can it even be an object? Puzzling, right? Yet somehow, such objects can be said to exist; massless particles exist.

Fact Snack

"Weight" is a gravity-based definition of mass, so your weight is different on every planet you visit. "Mass" is NOT gravity-based, so your mass is the same on every planet.

So I just need to go to the Moon to instantly lose weight!

Let's sc**ROOT**inise!

The curious thing about ALL atoms is that their mass is not distributed evenly. About 99.94% of the mass of an atom is found in the tiny nucleus.

Imagine if a small part of you, say the smallest toe on your left foot, weighed 70kg, and the rest of your body weighed a few grams.

It would be pretty tricky to go for a walk! Most of you would feel as light as a feather, but dragging that 70kg toe along would be hard work.

Now I see how an atom must find its nucleus to be a real drag.

This short book can't cover all the types of atoms and elements, but let's check out the rare earth elements. Despite the exclusive-sounding name, all these are metals that share one rather negative quality: when left in the open air, they get rusty like old cars left to rot outdoors. But they do have cool powers.

Remember the chart made by Mendeleev? Do you remember what it's called? (Hint: see page 43!) You can find the rare earth elements there. There's lanthanum and lutetium and scandium and yttrium, for example. Yes, the names are odd and some are hard to say, right? (For Yttrium, say i-tree-um.) But some have cool names, like promethium.

Fact Snack

Yttrium was named after the Swedish village in which it was discovered, Ytterby. Promethium was named after Prometheus, a legendary titan from Greek mythology, who gave the gift of fire to the mortals.

My present is hot stuff, like me.

Rare earth elements can be found in the crust layer of the Earth and also in seabeds and river beds. Because of their interesting powers, we can use them to make cool stuff. These range from high-powered lasers to revolutionary medical equipment to super-fast jet aircraft.

Let's sc**ROOT**inise!

A strange mineral was found in a mine in Sweden in 1751 and was set aside.

Thirty years later, the 15-year-old son of the mine's owner sent a sample to a materials expert, who couldn't work out if there was anything special about it.

But the young man, Wilhelm Hisinger, never forgot the odd rock and returned to re-examine it when he was a mining expert himself in his late 40s.

It turned out to be a new element in the rare earth category, which was eventually named cerium.

Moral of the story: If you can't find a good expert, you may have to spend a few years becoming the good expert.

To physicists, all atoms are fascinating, not just the rare ones because scientists know that the ways we harness their powers are important. These breakthroughs have changed our lives, affecting us every minute of every day.

How do gadgets work? What makes your phone or your handheld game or your computer function? How do your lights switch on or how does the water in your shower get heated? Yes, it's all due to the work that goes on inside atoms.

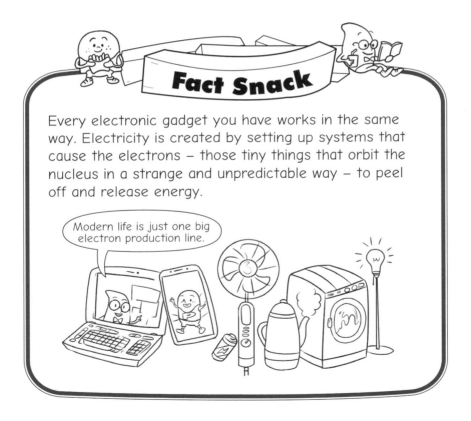

Fact Snack

Every electronic gadget you have works in the same way. Electricity is created by setting up systems that cause the electrons – those tiny things that orbit the nucleus in a strange and unpredictable way – to peel off and release energy.

Modern life is just one big electron production line.

If we set up our equipment so that this happens an unimaginably large number of times, we produce electrical current in power stations. We pump this through the city and into your home through the electricity outlets.

Some of it you feed straight into objects – the fridge, the washing machine, the TV. And some you put into a storage unit, like the battery of your phone, so that you can carry it around with you.

Almost all the cool gadget-related stuff that happens around you, from the ability to capture and play music, to the way you take photographs, to the way the Internet works, to the microwave oven that heats your dinner – it's all down to atoms.

Thanks, atoms!

If you want to know more about how electricity goes from atoms to the socket in your room, scan this QR code for an animated lesson.

Chapter 10
The future of atoms

What about the future? If this book interested you, you might want to find or make a new atom yourself. And if you do, you may even be able to name it after yourself or your dog or your hamster.

In principle, it is very simple. All you do is add an extra proton to the nucleus of an atom and it undergoes transmutation into a new one. Yes, you'd be doing the work of an alchemist. Perhaps you should get a pointy hat and a robe patterned with stars and moons to do it in!

Tater Toons

Before we set to work transmuting atoms, we need to note two challenges. First, reorganising elements is difficult because atoms are so small and fiddly. Second, new combinations don't hold together for long – in fact, they tend to fall apart in tiny fractions of a second. The people trying to make new atoms sometimes create something that had lasted for only a tiny amount of time, but it still gets added to the list.

But the biggest problem is that you may need a few hundred billion dollars to create the equipment. You may also need a big space too. We don't know how big your bedroom is, but it might not be large enough.

Many scientists search for atoms using the Large Hadron Collider, which is the biggest machine of any kind in the world. The main unit is an underground circular chamber, which is 27 kilometres in circumference, buried in the ground. It is so large that it actually stretches between two countries, France and Switzerland.

Scan this QR code to see a funny cartoon that lets you go on a journey around the tubes of CERN along with flying atoms.

Let's sc**ROOT**inise!

The magnets at the Large Hadron Collider need to be kept super-cold, so the machine is also the world's largest fridge. The temperature is super-super-super chilly, far lower than in the ultra-frozen areas of outer space beyond the solar system.

But at the same time, when it is switched on and working, it is one of the hottest places in the solar system! Parts of the system can reach temperatures hotter than the centre of the sun. It should get another prize for having the World's Most Contradictory Pair of Titles! How many places do you know that can be both extremely hot and extremely cold at the same time?

The protons that travel around the 27-km route move unimaginably fast, completing the circuit 11,000 times a second and they keep on going for many hours, racking up a journey of billions of kilometres in a single day.

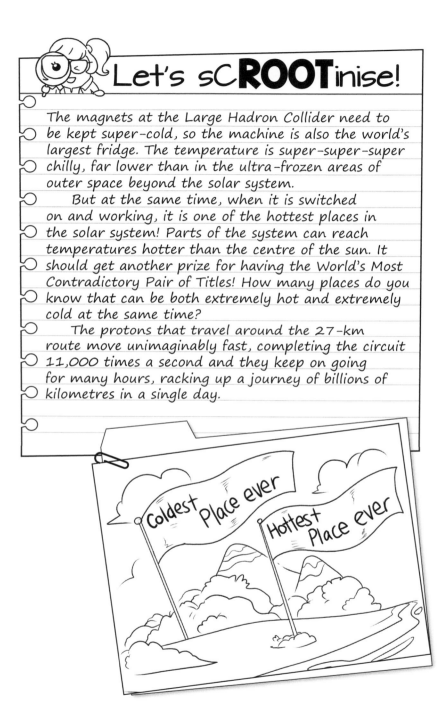

Coldest Place ever

Hottest Place ever

But are there simpler ways to do a bit of home transmuting of atoms or nuclear fission? In theory, yes. We did promise to show you how to split atoms at home, so here we go.

First, you need to get a bit of radium. These days many hospitals store radium, but they probably will be too sensible to give it out to people. In the old days, radium was painted onto watch hands and numbers to give them a green glow. But when people realised how dangerous it was in the 1970s, they stopped doing that. So radium is tricky to find.

Second, you need a bit of Uranium-235. Surprisingly, that may be easier to obtain. Some ordinary household smoke alarms have a tiny bit of the stuff inside.

You put the radium in a box with a tiny opening. Neutrons will fly out of the opening and, hopefully, hit your Uranium-235, splitting an atom and causing nuclear fission.

How likely is this to work? We have to be honest here: not very likely at all. And you know what? That's probably a good thing. Splitting atoms is probably best left to the experts. And we really wouldn't want you to blow up your home!

Fact Snack

When atoms are split in a nuclear power plant, the energy is released as heat. This is used to boil water to make steam, just like a giant version of your parents' tea kettle at home. The steam turns a turbine, which is a sort of engine that releases electrons, making a stream of electricity, which flows to homes for use, making light bulbs glow and gadgets work. All this infrastructure is provided just to make your light switch work.

Learning about atoms, the smallest things in the universe, curiously teaches us a lot about the largest things in the universe too: stars and star systems.

You'd think that galaxies are hugely complex places with countless substances and endless complexity, but they aren't.

One of the oddest things about the universe is that it is extremely simple. There is more complexity in your mother's cup of coffee than there is in the average star. A star is simply a big ball of one type of atom: hydrogen, the simplest atom of all.

Fact Snack

The word hydrogen comes from "hydro", which is Greek for "water", and "genes", which means "creating" as in The Book of Genesis. (Remember how shy Henry created water from hydrogen gas in 1766? See page 34 for the details.)

Thanks for the mention, but I'm still shy. Don't make a movie about me, okay?

Now other atoms, if we imagine them talking to each other on earth, might tease hydrogen for being boring.

Hydrogen is an atom with just the two essential parts and no extras. The nucleus has just one proton, and the fuzzy shell has just one electron (and that frequently goes missing).

But we should never be tempted to tease hydrogen atoms. If we count all the atoms in the whole universe, we will find that nine out of 10 are hydrogen atoms, three-quarters of all the mass (the stuff) in the universe is hydrogen atoms. So basically, we live in a universe of hydrogen atoms and should be respectful of them.

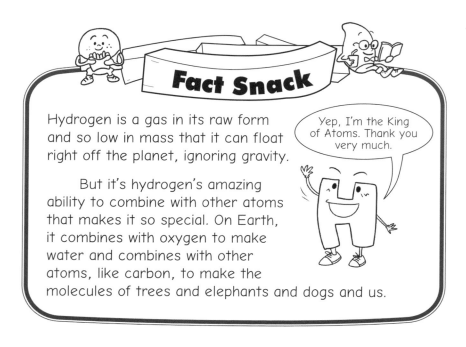

Fact Snack

Hydrogen is a gas in its raw form and so low in mass that it can float right off the planet, ignoring gravity.

Yep, I'm the King of Atoms. Thank you very much.

But it's hydrogen's amazing ability to combine with other atoms that makes it so special. On Earth, it combines with oxygen to make water and combines with other atoms, like carbon, to make the molecules of trees and elephants and dogs and us.

The smallest atom, as we said earlier, is the helium atom, which is also quite simple. The nucleus has two protons and one or two neutrons. Orbiting fuzzily are two electrons.

But the helium atom should also not be teased. We said above that three-quarters of the universe's mass is made of hydrogen atoms. Well, the vast majority of the rest of the atoms (about 25 percent) are helium atoms.

So the universe is made out of hydrogen and helium. All the remaining atoms added together make up only about one percent of the mass of the universe!

But that remainder part is important to us. It contains the famous carbon atoms, which are a key ingredient of human beings. In fact, about 99 percent of the human body is made up of a tiny number of elements. The Big Six are oxygen, carbon, hydrogen, nitrogen, calcium and phosphorus.

Let's sc**ROOT**inise!

Believe it or not, you've seen carbon atoms. They are what make lumps of coal into black, shiny things. They also make up the powdery black soot that results when things are burned to ashes.

But carbon's magical quality is the way it binds things together to form a surprisingly wide range of materials. So, for example, graphite (the black stuff in your pencil) comes from carbon. And if you take carbon's binding powers to their maximum level, the result is diamonds — the hardest objects on earth.

Fact Snack

If you weigh 60kg, 11kg is the weight of the carbon in your body.

The story of atoms started with the sage Aruni in India. At this point, approaching the end of our story, it makes sense to go back to where we started, to the Indian sages of ancient times. One of them said that "reality is a dream in the mind of God". It's a nice, poetic phrase, but doesn't sound very scientific, does it?

So, it's intriguing to find that the scientists who made the biggest contribution to the study of atoms, like Werner Heisenberg, were fascinated by ancient writings and believed they provided valuable insights into the nature of reality.

Many atomic scientists see an intriguing connection between consciousness and matter. This ranges from Heisenberg saying that matter "is made out of ideas", to modern science writers who say that what we know about atoms shows that all of physical reality is an illusion from inside our heads.

But even if that is so, you can't use that as an excuse to not do your homework or chores!

Tater Toons

We hope you've enjoyed *Atoms Everywhere!* and learnt something from it. If you have, it proves the truth of what we said at the start: atoms are amazing objects that have learnt to cluster into people-shaped groups and study themselves! Goodbye for now, from our atoms to your atoms.